Millie Marotta's
Curious
Creatures

First published in the United Kingdom in 2016 by
Batsford
1 Gower Street
London
WC1E 6HD

An imprint of Pavilion Books Group Ltd

Illustrations copyright © Millie Marotta Ltd, 2016
Volume copyright © Batsford, 2016

ISBN: 9781849943659

A CIP catalogue record for this book is available
from the British Library.

20 19 18 17 16 15 16
10 9 8 7 6 5 4 3 2 1

Repro by Mission, Hong Kong
Printed by GPS, Bosnia

This book can be ordered direct from the publisher at the website:
www.pavilionbooks.com, or try your local bookshop.

Millie Marotta's

Curious Creatures

a colouring book adventure

BATSFORD

Introduction

If you are familiar with any of my previous colouring books you will know that I am somewhat fascinated by the animal kingdom. From a very young age I was utterly captivated by the marvels of our natural world and I feel incredibly privileged that my work allows me to combine my love of drawing with my passion for wildlife.

With *Curious Creatures* being my fourth colouring book, I would like to say that the process of selecting which animals will be included becomes a little easier, but it really doesn't. There are just so many amazing creatures out there to choose from, each with its own unique characteristics and qualities – and this is where the idea for *Curious Creatures* came from. For this book I decided to bring together a collection of animals that I find quite remarkable, slightly peculiar, unusual, quirky or even a little strange. But all quite beautiful to me.

It was still very hard to narrow it down to those that eventually made the pages of the book, but in the end I settled on some of my favourites. From flamboyant show-offs to masters of camouflage, this book brings together a rich array of intriguing birds, fish, mammals, amphibians, reptiles and invertebrates for you to enjoy and colour to your heart's content. Some were chosen for their bizarre behaviour, others for their unusual physical appearance or even for their incredible survival skills. From the Amazonian royal flycatcher with its flamboyant feathered headdress to the magical flying fish. From the splendour of the lion's mane jellyfish to the downright bizarre yet utterly charming duck-billed platypus.

My illustrations always begin as quite realistic drawings of the creatures, keeping the form of the animal very much true to life. I then begin to elaborate, building up lots of detail by adding intricate patterns and ornate embellishments, resulting in a collection of real creatures with a creative twist. From time to time readers ask me about specific animals in previous books. With that in mind and given that some of the animals in *Curious Creatures* might be a little less obvious, I have decided to include a 'contents page', listing each animal in the order they appear, which you will find at the back of the book. While a great many of you like to let your imagination run wild when choosing your colours, there are others who like to create something that is more true to life, so I hope this list helps those of you who might want to research the animals a little before diving in with your colours. What I love about creating these books is that not only do I get to bring together my two passions in life – nature and drawing – I also get to share the experience with you, the reader. Seeing my black-and-white line drawings brought to life with colour and watching how differently you each go about turning these images into something of your own is incredibly exciting and tremendously inspiring.

I am thrilled to see how colouring has been embraced across the world and has become a regular activity for so many people. I continue to be amazed by the colouring community and how enthusiastic, passionate and involved you are. On a daily basis I see what I can frankly only describe as ridiculously beautiful examples of coloured pages from my books being shared over social media – people are running clubs and competitions, providing online tutorials, sharing colouring tips and talking about materials and techniques. A whole community has come together over colouring and I think that is a wonderful thing.

Occasionally I'm asked how a particular image should be coloured, or which materials, colours or techniques should be used. My answer is always the same – there is no right or wrong way and there are no rules. Each one of you will colour in your own unique way. You will have your own thoughts and ideas about how you choose to work with the illustrations and it is this individual approach that makes these images ultimately become your own art works.

For those of you who enjoy adding your own drawings to the illustrations as well as colouring them, I have scattered a few images amongst the pages that are less detailed than most, leaving empty space for you to add your own drawn details, textures and patterns. I have also included some blank pages at the back of the book, which you might like to use for drawing your own curious creatures or for testing out new colours and materials.

However you like to colour, whatever materials you choose to use and whatever techniques you like to explore, I really hope you enjoy the illustrations in this book. I can't wait to see how differently each of you will flood these pages with colour, bringing to life your very own vibrant world of curious creatures.

Millie Marotta

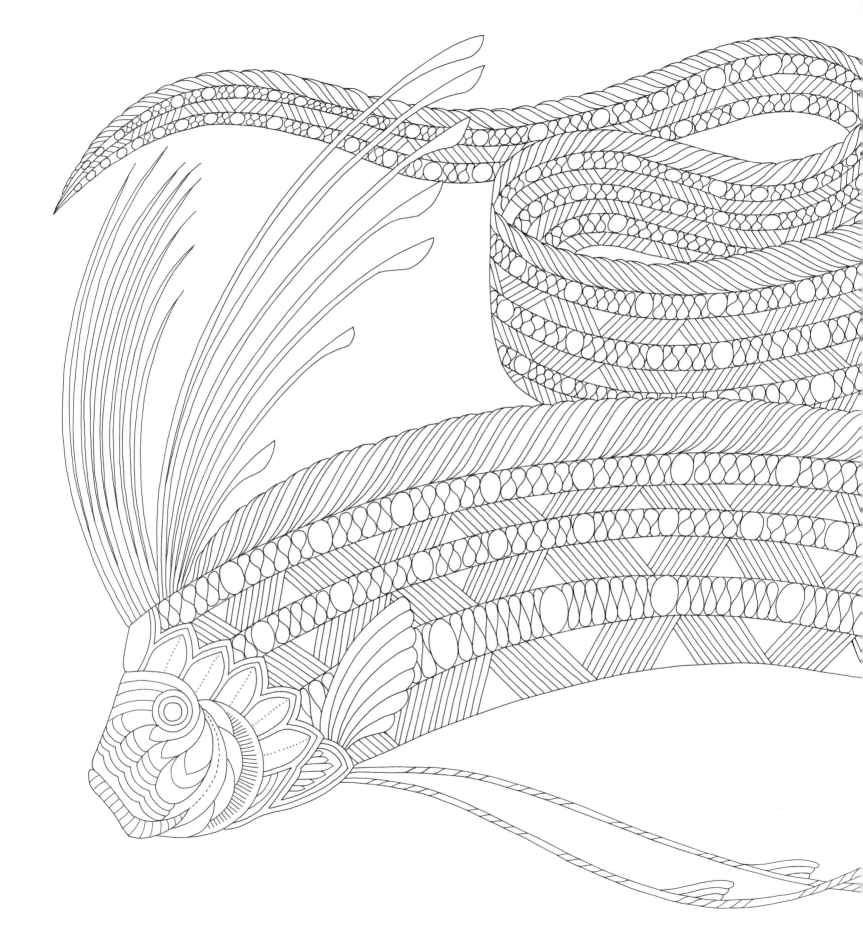

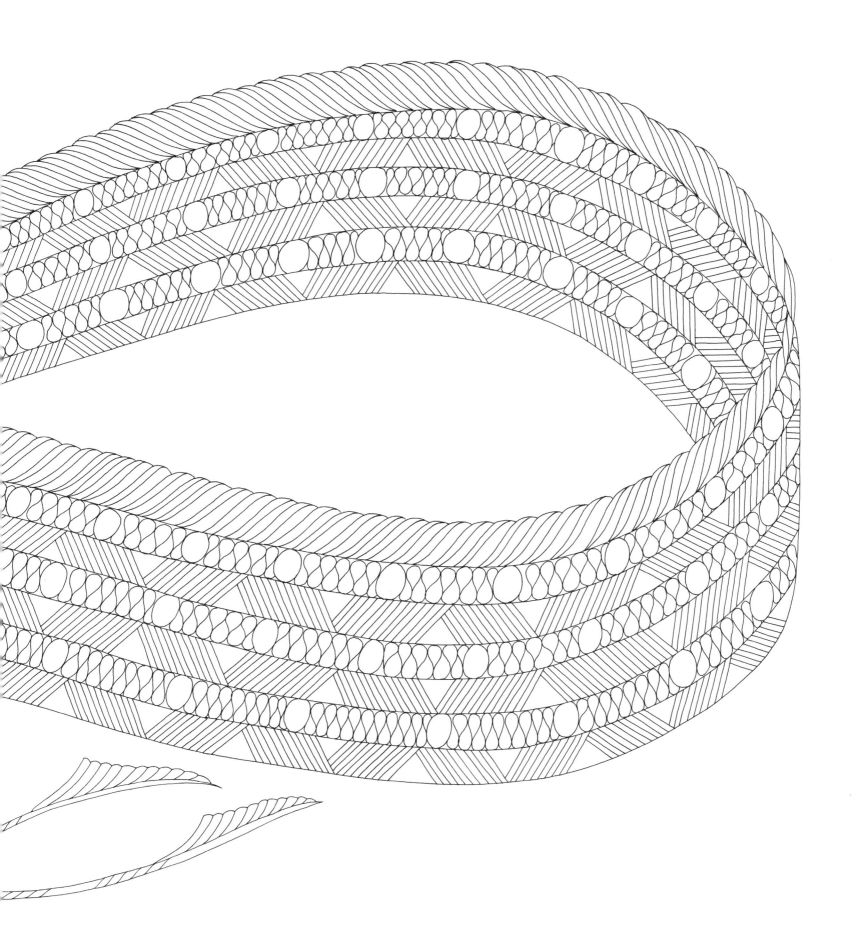

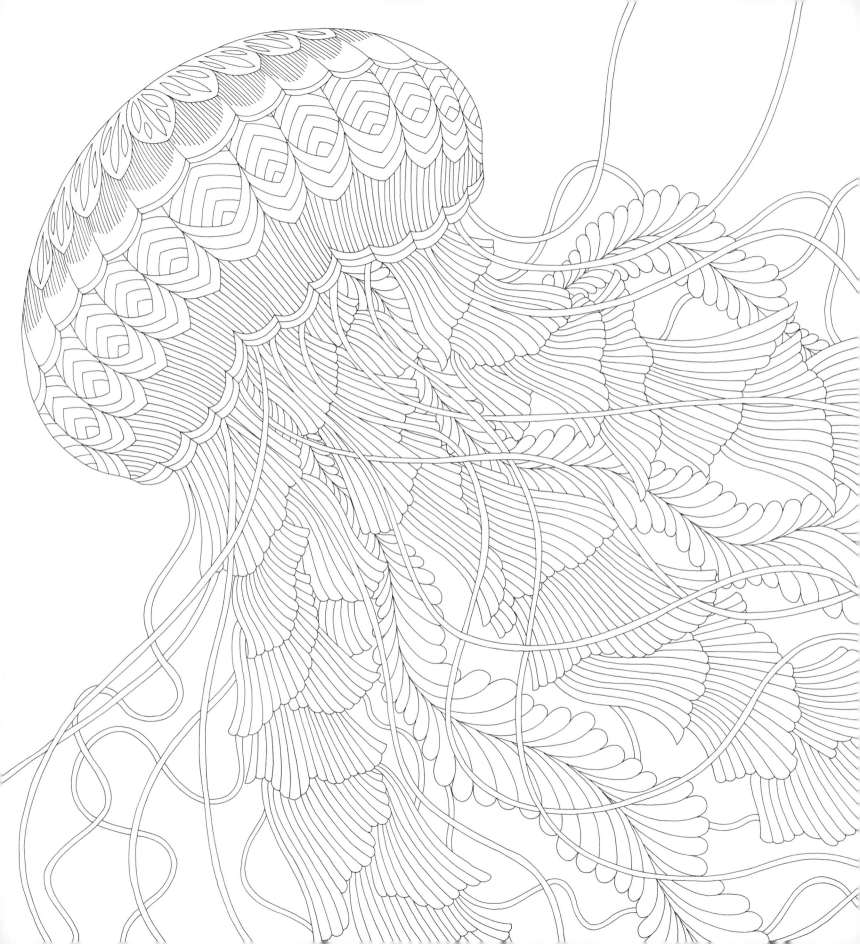

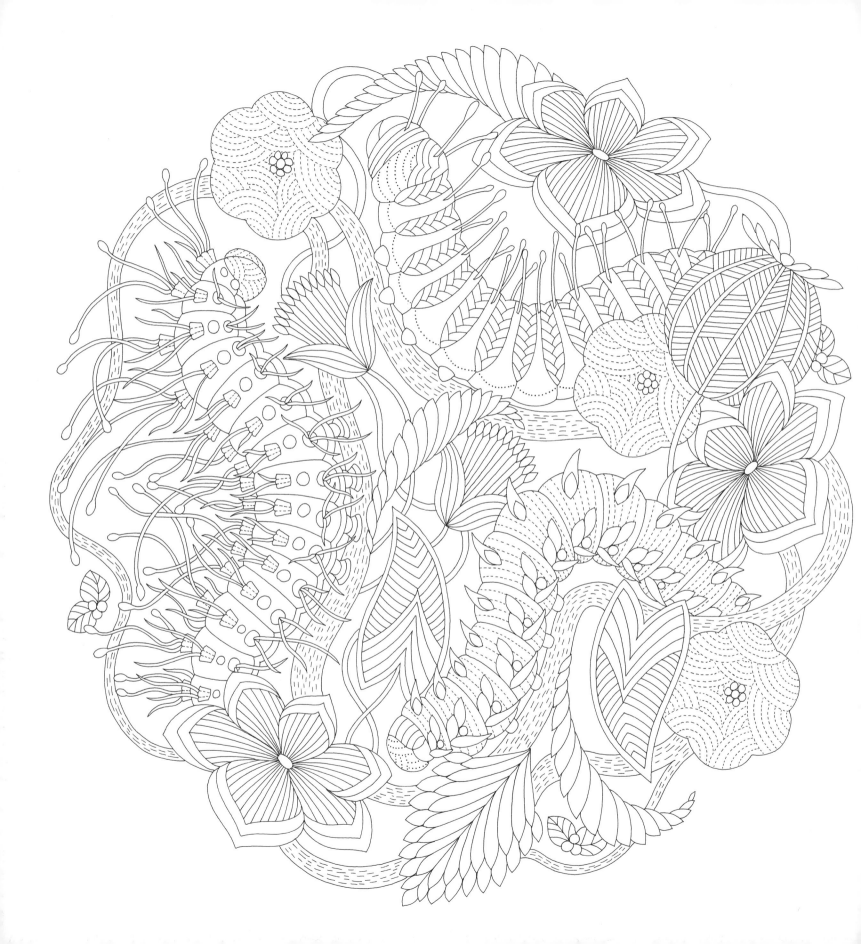

Create your own curious creatures here…

Curious Creatures

Flying fish
Exocoetidae

Coconut crab
Birgus latro

Giant oarfish
Regalecus glesne

Duck-billed platypus
Ornithorhynchus anatinus

Beaver
Castor

Narwhal
Monodon monoceros

Plumed Basilisk lizard
Basiliscus plumifrons

Rajah Brooke's Birdwing
  butterfly
Trogonoptera brookiana

Poison dart frogs
Dendrobatidae

Amazonian royal flycatcher
*Onychorhynchus coronatus
  coronatus*

Praying mantis
Mantodea

Scalloped hammerhead
  shark
Sphyrna lewini

Northern gannet
Morus bassanus

Gerenuk
Litocranius walleri

Mandarinfish
Synchiropus splendidus
Dragon wrasse
Novaculichthys taeniourus

Chinese water deer
Hydropotes inermis inermis

Axolotl
Ambystoma mexicanum

Sea anemones
Actiniaria
Giant clam
Tridacna gigas
Sea sponge
Porifera
Christmas tree worms
Spirobranchus giganteus
Coral
Anthozoa

Bactrian camel
Camelus bactrianus

Fennec fox
Vulpes zerda

Giant squid
Architeuthis

Patagonian mara
Dolichotis patagonum

King-of-Saxony bird-of-
  paradise
Pteridophora alberti

Hummingbird
  hawk-moth
Macroglossum stellatarum

Devil lionfish
Pterois miles

Manta ray
Manta birostris

May bug
Melolontha melolontha

Sailfish
Istiophorus platypterus

Macaroni penguin
Eudyptes chrysolophus

Malayan tapir
Tapirus indicus

Hermit crab
Paguroidea

Peacock mantis shrimp
Odontodactylus scyllarus

American white pelicans
Pelecanus erythrorhynchos

Sea urchins
Echinoidea

Mimic octopus
Thaumoctopus mimicus

Chambered nautilus
Nautilus pompilius

Weedy sea dragon
Phyllopteryx taeniolatus

Blue-footed booby
Sula nebouxii

Elephant shrew
Macroscelididae

Okapi
Okapia johnstoni

Tufted puffin
Fratercula cirrhata

Black-throated loon
Gavia arctica

Rhinoceros hornbill
Buceros rhinoceros

Crested porcupine
Hystrix cristata

Rosy maple moth
Dryocampa rubicunda
Chinese moon moth
Actias dubernardi
Luna moth
Actias luna
Indonesian owl moth
Brahmaea hearseyi
Poplar hawk-moth
Laothoe populi

Greater prairie chicken
Tympanuchus cupido

Shoebill
Balaeniceps rex

Yeti crab
Kiwa hirsute

Pygmy seahorses
Hippocampus bargibanti

Nudibranchs
Nudibranchia

Jewel beetles
Temognatha alternata

Longhorn cowfish
Lactoria cornuta

Pipefish
Syngnathinae

Kiwi
Apteryx

Mandarin duck
Aix galericulata

Lion's mane jellyfish
Cyanea capillata

Walrus
Odobenus rosmarus

Moose
Alces alces

Amazonian leaf-footed bug
Diactor bilineatus

Cuttlefish
Sepiida

Giant Peacock moth
    caterpillar
Saturnia pyri
Joseph's Coat moth
    caterpillar
Agarista agricola
Southern Marbled Emperor
    moth caterpillar
Heniocha apollonia

Great grey owl
Strix nebulosa

Long-eared jerboa
Euchoreutes naso

Brown-throated sloth
Bradypus variegatus

Golden pheasant
Chrysolophus pictus

Tibetan sand fox
Vulpes ferrilata

Jackson's chameleon
Trioceros jacksonii

To find out more about these curious creatures
and why I find them so intriguing visit
millliemarotta.co.uk/CreatureCuriosities